Battle Stations!

FORTIFICATIONS THROUGH THE AGES

BY STEPHEN SHAPIRO
ART BY MEI TSAO
AND KEN NICE

Annick Press
Toronto • New York • Vancouver

Many thanks to Ken Nice who reconstructed whole buildings from ruins and
diagrams, and to Mei Tsao who gave the structures color, drama, and life.
—Stephen Shapiro

Annick Press Ltd.

We acknowledge the support of the Canada Council for the Arts, the Ontario
Arts Council, and the Government of Canada through the Book Publishing
Industry Development Program (BPIDP) for our publishing activities.

Cataloging in Publication

Shapiro, Stephen, date-
Battle stations! : fortifications through the ages / by Stephen
Shapiro ; art by Mei Tsao and Ken Nice.

Includes index.
ISBN 1-55037-888-0 (pbk.).—ISBN 1-55037-889-9 (bound)

1. Fortification—History—Juvenile literature. I. Tsao, Mei
II. Nice, Ken III. Title.

UG405.S46 2005   j355.7'09   C2004-906701-X

The art in this book was drafted in pen and ink, scanned, and then colored electronically.
The text was typeset in Trajan and Apollo.

Distributed in Canada by:	Published in the U.S.A. by Annick Press (U.S.) Ltd.
Firefly Books Ltd.	Distributed in the U.S.A. by:
66 Leek Crescent	Firefly Books (U.S.) Inc.
Richmond Hill, ON	P.O. Box 1338
L4B 1H1	Ellicott Station
	Buffalo, NY 14205

Printed in China.

Visit us at: www.annickpress.com

Measurements normally appear in metric with imperial measurements following in parentheses. An exception is made where gun calibers were designated
by the manufacturer in imperial.

To my family for their
support and advice.
—S.S.

In memory of my mother.
—M.T.

To my mother for a lifetime
of support.
—K.N.

Some of the fortifications in this book, as well as many others, are operated as tourist attractions. Of
course, the Great Wall of China draws tourists from around the world. Many Japanese castles have
either survived, such as Himeji Castle, or been reconstructed, like Kakegawa Castle. All over Europe
there are many accessible surviving fortresses. A number of Martello towers in Great Britain and
around the world have been preserved. Several can be visited in Kingston and Halifax, Canada.
Preserved coast defense batteries can be found all around America, such as at Key West (Fort
Zachary Taylor) and San Francisco (in Golden Gate Park). Not all forts have been converted into
museums or protected as historic sites. I was once surprised to discover a fort in the middle of a golf
course! Always be careful when exploring old fortifications.

—Stephen Shapiro

CONTENTS

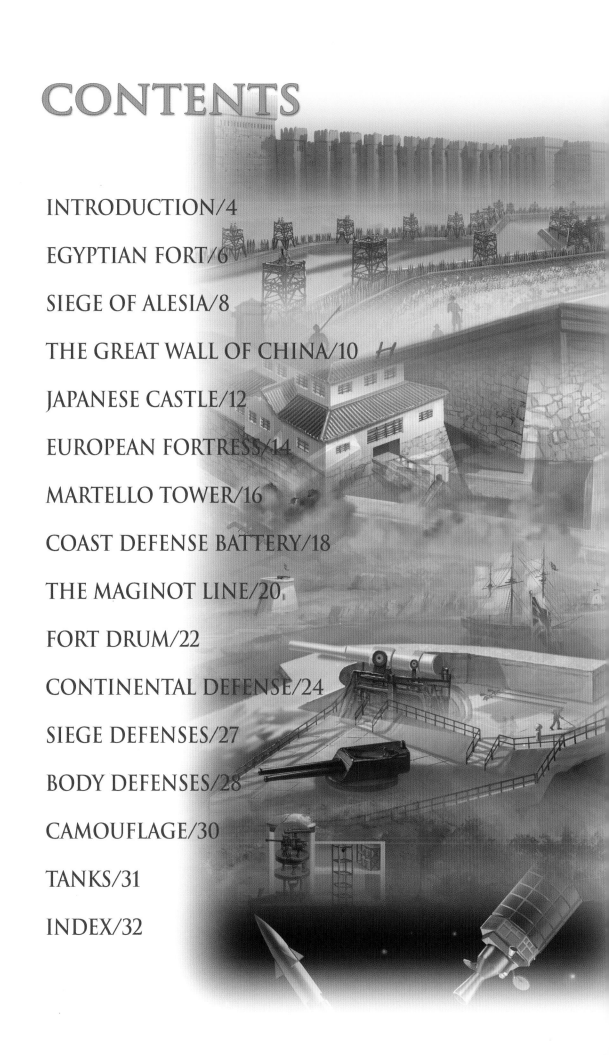

THROUGHOUT HISTORY, war has brought devastation to countless people, their environment, and their hopes and aspirations. Leaders have always tried to find ways to protect soldiers, resources, and civilians from destruction. One solution is to keep them out of harm's way – in fortifications.

FORTIFICATIONS HAVE EXISTED SINCE THE DAWN OF HUMAN SETTLEMENT in almost every place around the globe. African villages surrounded themselves with walls of thorn bushes, Neolithic Europeans with deep ditches, and New Zealand Maori with palisades of timber. Jericho, one of the oldest cities in the world, had a sturdy wall as thick as four people standing side by side. In fact, most early cities – from Europe to Asia – featured stout defensive walls.

OF COURSE, FORTIFICATIONS HAVE CHANGED OVER TIME. As warfare evolved, fortresses had to grow bigger, tougher, and more complex. Wooden palisades became stone towers, brick bastions, then concrete bunkers. Today a nation can be "fortified" with satellites and radars. As humans have created more advanced technologies of destruction, fortifications have been forced to keep pace.

The invention of the cannon made it a lot easier for besiegers to send a medieval castle's tall and thin stone walls crashing down. Fortress designers responded with lower, thicker walls – much harder to destroy with cannon.

The development of high-angle artillery and explosive shells drove fortifications underground. The 20th-century forts of the Maginot Line were buried under 20 m (65 feet) of soil to protect them from those crushing bombardments. Only their gun turrets rose above the surface.

THE ROLES THAT FORTRESSES PLAY IN WARFARE HAVE VARIED. Fortifications have served as refuges from attack (the Japanese castle), customs posts (forts on the Egyptian frontier), port defenses (Fort Drum in Manila Bay), or even protection for an entire country (Great Wall of China). Despite all this change, however, the principles of fortification have remained the same. Every fort must keep its enemies out. A fortress that cannot protect itself is useless. It must be able to resist bombardment from a distance, assault from close up, and even a surprise attack. One 18th-century fortress fell to a dramatic ruse: officers from the attacking French army disguised themselves as women, seized a gate, and let their army into the town.

EVEN IF A FORTRESS IS SECURE, IT STILL MAY NOT ACHIEVE ITS PURPOSE. The Great Wall of China resisted nomadic attacks but was too expensive for a dynasty in decline to maintain. The island of Fort Drum was practically indestructible, but the city it defended was conquered from another direction – the land.

Although they are generally no longer brick, stone, or concrete, fortifications still exist in every country. And they will probably be around for a long time to come. While we hope for an end to war – when fortifications will finally become historical curiosities – they continue to consume human ingenuity and great sums of money, all with the hope that it's possible to stay one good idea ahead of the enemy.

Glossary

Artillery: Guns that shoot large shells.

Barracks: A building where soldiers live.

Battery: A group of artillery pieces, either in the field or in a fortification.

Casemate: A strongly built room with an opening from which a weapon can be fired.

Garrison: The troops who guard a location.

Moat: A ditch, usually filled with water, that protects a fortification.

Mortar: An artillery piece that shoots almost vertically. A mortar's shells go high over obstacles and can hit enemies sheltering behind them.

Siege: The surrounding of a fortified place in order to cut off help and then capture it.

Turret: A rotating structure that protects a gun inside it but still allows the gun to fire in any direction.

EGYPTIAN FORT

Marvelous treasures were brought to Egypt from the south – from the lands of Nubia and Kush. Heavily laden merchant boats carried them down the river Nile to palaces in the capital, Thebes. The pharaoh, divine ruler of Egypt, declared that only he was allowed to import these exotic goods into the country.

Egypt was a rich and well-protected land. To the east and west were harsh, impassible deserts. To the north was the wide Mediterranean Sea. In the south, at the rapids called the Second Cataract, a group of colossal forts barred the way into Egypt.

The forts did more than protect Egypt's southern frontier. Guards there prevented any trade taking place without the pharaoh's permission. Gold, ivory, exotic animals, and slaves all passed under the watchful eyes of Egyptian guards.

The inspection was only possible because the Second Cataract's swift and turbulent rapids were too dangerous to sail through. Instead, goods needed to be unloaded and carried past the rapids on land. These shipments were inspected by Egyptian officers from the forts before they were reloaded on new boats and sent on to Egypt.

Obviously, such treasures attracted unwelcome attention. Soldiers stood guard on fortress walls, and local tribesmen were paid to watch for raiding parties. Any bandits who tried to interfere with Egyptian trade would be crushed with an iron fist.

These enormous forts didn't need to be as large as they were just to protect goods from raiders, or Egypt from the local tribes. They were built on such a massive scale to serve as a declaration of Egyptian power. Their names, like "Subduer of Nubia" or "Curbing the Foreign Countries," served the same purpose. The forts guarded Egypt's borders, Egypt's goods, and Egypt's pride.

GATEHOUSE
The main gate of the fort was flanked by two large towers that extended well beyond the gate itself. They formed a narrowing passage that forced attackers to approach the gate one at a time. Right in front of the gate was a drawbridge that could be pulled back on wooden rollers to reveal a pit.

WALLS AND TOWERS

The walls of the Egyptian forts were made from mud bricks that were shaped by hand, then left in the hot desert sun to dry and harden.

The walls were pierced with openings through which soldiers could fire arrows or throw stones. In addition, most forts had a lower outer wall as a first line of defense.

Large towers stood at the corners of each wall, with smaller ones along the sides.

ARMIES OF THE PHARAOHS

Egyptian soldiers rarely had to fight invaders. They wore no armor, preferring instead only a short linen kilt. For protection they carried rectangular shields made from hardened leather, and they fought with axes, spears, and bows.

WATER SUPPLY

The Egyptians were careful to make sure that they would have fresh water even during a siege. Each fort had a set of covered stairs or a tunnel that led down to the Nile. That way, they could draw water from the river even if they were totally surrounded.

WATER SUPPLY

Nile River

Egypt

Thebes •

Nubia and Kush

Second Cataract

THE NILE

Egypt was a fertile country because of the Nile River. Every year, the Nile overflowed its banks. When the waters receded, rich soil was left behind. The Nile was also the fastest and easiest way to travel through the country. You could sail up the river, then let the current carry you back down on your return journey.

SIEGE OF ALESIA

The mighty Roman legions crushed every enemy they faced. Proud Greeks, fanatical Celto-Iberians, and other cultures from Spain to the Black Sea had all been forced to bow before the soldier-engineers known as "Marius' Mules" (because of the heavy loads the general Marius had made each Roman legionary carry).

In 59 BCE a young Roman aristocrat named Julius Caesar was appointed governor of Roman Gaul (now southern France). Caesar was energetic and ruthless, like many other Roman generals before him. He invaded independent Gaul (northern France), conquering its tribes over the next six years. In desperation, several tribes revolted against Roman rule. They chose as their leader an inspiring Gallic chieftain named Vercingetorix.

After a few minor victories, the rebellious Gauls were defeated in battle. Caesar pursued them to the fortified hilltop town of Alesia. Unsure that he could successfully storm the city, Caesar decided to starve the rebels into surrender.

He immediately ordered his legionaries to begin erecting a line of fortifications around the hill. The combination of walls, ditches, and traps would prevent anyone bringing food into the town. More importantly, it would stop the warriors inside from breaking out of Caesar's trap. Once the first line of defenses was complete, Caesar began to build a second line of fortifications outside the first. These were on the other side of the Romans, and faced away from Alesia. Vercingetorix had many allies, and the walls would prevent another Gallic army from attacking the besiegers in the rear.

No sooner were these walls complete than a relieving army arrived outside Alesia. After a few nerve-racking days, the army outside the wall attacked the Romans. Seeing this, the men in Alesia joined the assault, but both were repulsed by the disciplined Roman soldiers. A second assault also failed. Finally, Vercingetorix admitted defeat. He and his men surrendered to the Romans. Gaul would remain a Roman province for almost 500 years.

CAESAR'S LEGIONS
Roman legions in Caesar's time consisted of paid volunteers. Each soldier had a short thrusting sword and a heavy javelin called a *pilum*, as well as a shield, helmet, and body armor. The pilum was designed to bend when it hit an enemy's shield so it couldn't be pulled out. This unbalanced the shield and made it useless. The well-trained Roman soldiers then finished the attack with their thrusting swords.

The inner wall was 16 km (10 miles) long and the outer one 28 km (17 miles).

INNER DITCH

THE GAULS
Although Roman writers described them as brutish barbarians, the Gauls had a highly developed culture. They divided themselves into tribes along family lines. The Gauls produced beautiful crafts, particularly metalwork. Gallic warriors fought from horseback or on foot, using a wide variety of swords, spears, and javelins. Fanatical warriors showed their bravery by going without armor and painting themselves in bright colors.

RAMPARTS

The Roman soldiers stood guard on towers that rose from an earthen rampart with a ditch immediately in front. Sharpened stakes pointed out horizontally between the rampart and the wooden wall on top, to stop anyone trying to climb out of the ditch. Towers stood every 25 m (82 feet) along the wall – a quarter of the length of a soccer field. Well in front of the wall was a further pair of ditches, one filled with water and the other dry.

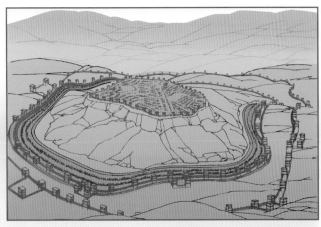

Two lines of Roman fortifications encircled the Gallic town of Alesia (center) – preventing either escape or reinforcement.

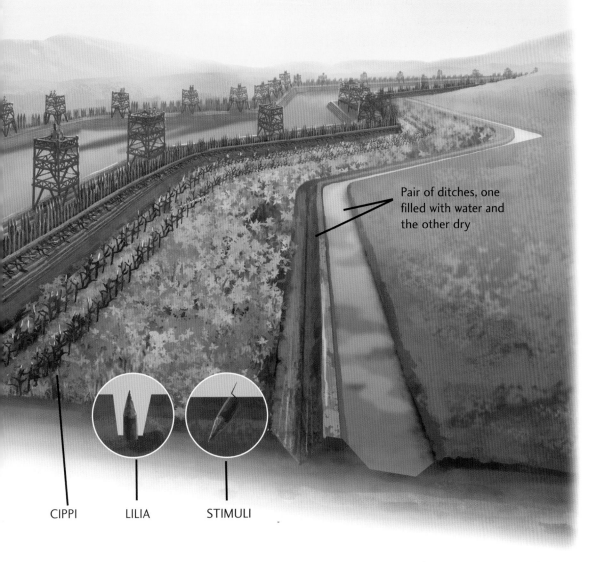

Pair of ditches, one filled with water and the other dry

CIPPI   LILIA   STIMULI

OBSTACLES

Between the outer pair of ditches and the inner ditch was a "garden" of obstacles intended to slow the Gauls down.

Furthest out were the Stimuli, iron spikes stuck into blocks of wood, then buried so only a few centimeters were above-ground. Next came the

Lilia, or Lilies, rows of hidden pits with wooden stakes pointing upwards. Finally came the Cippi, entire bushes with all their branches sharpened that were "planted" in the ground.

All these things could be avoided by alert Gauls, but they were slowed or halted long enough for the Romans to kill them with javelins or arrows.

9

THE GREAT WALL OF CHINA

It's easy to build a wall to protect a town. But how do you build a wall that protects an entire country? This was a problem that the Han Dynasty of China had to solve. The nomadic Hsiung-nu were raiding China, pillaging and plundering, and the Han couldn't stop them.

The Hsiung-nu lived to the north, on the great grasslands of Mongolia. Their lifestyle took them from camp to camp, following their herds. They had no towns, mines, or workshops, so there were plenty of things that they couldn't make – like silk or metal. They raided China to obtain these things.

The Chinese tried to negotiate. They opened markets where the nomads could buy grain and luxuries. They married a Chinese princess to the leader of the nomads, and declared the Chinese and the Hsiung-nu "brothers." They gave the nomads gifts of silk, grain, and wine. Trade and bribes prevented some raids, but not all.

The Chinese tried going on the offensive. They sent armies into the grasslands where the nomads lived. The nomads simply retreated; they had no towns to defend. When the Chinese armies were exhausted, the Hsiung-nu surrounded and quickly defeated them.

When everything else had failed, the Chinese chose the only other way they could think of to keep the nomads from bringing terror to China. Piece by piece, they constructed a long wall along their northern border.

A wall this long could not be guarded everywhere—a few nomads might sneak over. But soldiers in watchtowers could see large groups of nomads approaching. They would then summon reinforcements to stop the Hsiung-nu.

When properly maintained, the Great Wall brought peace to the border. However, as domestic troubles forced the dynasty into decline, the wall fell into disrepair. Without soldiers or repairs, it became useless against the nomads.

The wall built by the Han Dynasty was not the first or the last Great Wall of China. Many dynasties, both before and after the Han, built their own Great Wall along the same border. To save time and money, they often used parts of older walls.

The current Great Wall was built by the Ming Dynasty in the 16th century, 1,500 years after the Han dynasty. It is the only man-made object that can be seen from space.

WATCHTOWER

BUILDING THE WALL
Chinese walls were made of packed earth. A wooden frame with no top or bottom was placed on the ground. It was filled with earth, which was pounded hard by workers' feet then covered with a layer of bamboo stems. Then the wooden frame was lifted off and placed on top, and a new layer of dirt poured in. Each layer was roughly 10 cm (4 inches) high, and a wall could have up to 150 layers. A single man could build a stretch of wall 5.5 m (18 feet) long in a month.

WATCHTOWERS

The Han built a line of watch-towers behind the Great Wall. Five to ten soldiers lived in rooms at the base and stood guard on a platform at the top. From there, soldiers could also send messages from tower to tower using colored flags, smoke, or torches. Isolated from the rest of the country, guard duty was lonely work.

THE GREAT WALL

The Han Dynasty Great Wall was over 6,000 km (3,728 miles) long. The wall was constructed with all sorts of local building materials and techniques. Stone was frequently used in the mountains, a mix of sand and tamarisk branches in the desert, and one province even used oak boards.

THE NOMADS

Nomads are people who have no permanent home, but travel from place to place raising their flocks of animals. The Hsiung-nu learned to ride and shoot a bow with great skill. They made excellent fighters when riding their small, tough ponies.

Nomads move from place to place looking for grass for their herds. They never stay long in the same spot, which means they can't grow vegetables or grain – which both require constant care.

SOLDIERS OF THE WALL

The Han armies were made up of conscripts, regular farmers who were required to serve in the army for two years and could be called up again in an emergency. Specially trained conscripts served as cavalry or crossbow-men. At the wall, the conscripts manned watchtowers, trained, and repaired the wall.

JAPANESE CASTLE

Feuding lords ruled 16th-century Japan. Order had collapsed. Anyone with a handful of armed men could take over a small valley and declare himself a *daimyo* – a word that literally meant "big man." The smallest of these daimyo were little more than bandits. To avoid being conquered by another daimyo, a lord needed a stronghold.

The first castles were built on the tops of hills and mountains. From that height, even a minor daimyo could defend himself against a much stronger force. His farmers could hide in the castle when invaders ravaged the land. More powerful daimyo built their castles down on the plains to be closer to the fields they ruled. Being lower down made their castles less secure, but their larger armies made up for this. The castles of the largest daimyo were more than just strongholds. Thriving towns grew up outside their walls to serve the *samurai* (warriors) who lived there.

Building on the plains presented special problems. The hills were smaller, and in some places didn't exist at all. The daimyos were forced to make artificial hills, then build their castles on top. These hills made terrible bases. If the castle on top was too heavy, the hill would collapse. The solution was to enclose the hill in its own thick stone walls. A bigger castle, with a much bigger keep, could be built on a stone-walled base.

Daimyo preferred to capture castles without a fight. They might bribe the defenders – offering power or money – or try to starve them out. If this did not succeed, their samurai would scale the walls of the castle and cross swords with the defenders. One of the most unusual ways of taking a castle was to divert a nearby river and create a flood, forcing the defenders to surrender.

Eventually, after 150 years of feuding, the great general Tokugawa Ieyasu forged powerful alliances, defeated the rest of the daimyo, and made himself ruler of all Japan. He made all the daimyo his subjects, retaining them as governors of their old lands. Tokugawa forbade the construction of any new castles, which kept the daimyo weak. His dynasty, called the Tokugawa shogunate, lasted over 250 years.

1580 CE

HIDDEN FLOOR
Many keeps (see facing page) contained a "hidden floor" to disguise the tower's capacity and confuse an attacker. The pagoda appeared to have three stories when viewed from the outside, but actually had four. Here, the third floor is hidden by a roof.

MOATS
Moats provided an extra barrier attackers had to cross.

KEEP

The central tower of the castle (called the *tenshu kaku*) sat at the highest point, on its own stone base.

Constructed like a pagoda, with a central supporting beam, it contained most of the castle's living space.

Because the tenshu was made of wood, its topmost roof was crowned by metal dolphins (*shachi*) to protect against evil fire spirits. More practically, the tenshu was coated with fire-resistant plaster or lacquer.

NINJAS

Ninjas were Japanese warriors who were specially trained in spying and assassination.

The castle's windows were covered with iron grates and surrounded by spikes to protect them from ninjas.

Inside the castle, certain floors were designed so they creaked when walked upon. They were called "Nightingale" floors, since the sound the floor made was similar to a nightingale's song.

GATES

Access to the keep was via a series of courtyards (called *maru*). The route through these courtyards involved multiple twists and turns to slow enemies and prevent them finding the next gate. Some castles had more than 20 gates.

ISHI OTOSHI

ISHI OTOSHI

To protect against attackers climbing up the stone base, walls and towers were provided with overhangs where stones could be dropped on enemies below. These protrusions (called *ishi otoshi*) were closed by wooden doors when not in use.

WALLS

A Japanese castle's walls were made from plaster and ground rock. Openings were provided for the warriors to shoot through: triangular for guns and rectangular for bows.

13

EUROPEAN FORTRESS

The invention of gunpowder changed the world of fortification with a bang. The age of the knight was ending. Kings began to experiment with a strange new weapon called the cannon. Too large and unwieldy to use on the battlefield – a team of oxen could drag one only 5 km (3 miles) in an entire day – cannon excelled at smashing the tall, thin walls of castles with solid shot.

A dramatic change was needed to protect the princes of Europe. Starting in the middle of the 16th century, newer fortresses were built with lower, thicker walls. These would be harder to send crashing down. However, lower walls were easier for attackers to scale. Inventive engineers constructed deep ditches in front of their fortress's walls, making them almost impossible to climb.

The ditches brought new problems. The depth of the ditch and the thickness of the wall meant that attackers lurking at the base of the wall were out of sight. The guards needed towers that would project outward from the wall to solve the problem. But both square and round towers still had blind spots where attacking troops could hide. Designers invented a new, unusual shape for towers, which they called a *bastion*. All of this combined to form a new style of fortification perfected over the next 150 years. Stopped in their tracks by these improved fortresses, kings had to find better ways to conquer them!

The first step of their new strategy was to dig a series of shallow zig-zag trenches towards the fortress. Once the attackers finally reached the ditch, they would place their cannon on the edge and batter a hole in the fortress's wall. Now the garrison's chances of victory were slim. If they surrendered, they would be free to leave; if not, they'd be put to the sword when the fortress was captured. Surrendering was common.

The entire siege could take several months, or even longer. The Spanish siege of Ostend took three years, three months, three weeks, three days, and three hours. The destructive power of cannon had turned war into an endless series of sieges.

CITADEL
A town's *citadel*, a fortress within a fortress, had many purposes. As well as being part of the main fortifications, it was both a final refuge if the besiegers broke into the town and also protection for the town garrison from rebellious townspeople.

CITADEL

GLACIS
A smooth, shallow slope called the *glacis* surrounded the fortress. Cleared of all houses, bushes, or trees, it left nowhere for attackers to hide. Because of the glacis's slope, the attacker's cannon had to be placed right on the edge of the ditch to hit the fortress walls.

Low walls were thicker and harder to hit with cannon. A deep ditch in front made them difficult to climb.

OUTERWORK

Parts of the fortress outside the main ditch were called *outerworks*. These protected important suburbs, river crossings, or hills that could not be enclosed in the main defenses. Each outerwork had its own bastions, ditch, and glacis.

Square and round towers had blind spots where enemies could hide (the shaded areas in the top drawing). The bastion, shown below, had none.

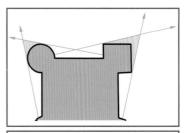

OUTERWORK

RAVELIN

Ravelins were triangular fortifications that sat in the fortress's ditch. Their guns could fire into the ditch or out over the glacis.

TRENCHES

Gunfire from the fortress walls, and from infantry on the outer edge of the ditch (called the *covered way*), meant that attackers had to dig trenches in the glacis to reach the ditch. The trenches zig-zagged so cannonballs couldn't bounce down the entire length of the trench.

MARTELLO TOWER

General Napoleon Bonaparte dreamed of conquering all of Europe. The troops of his French Empire had crushed all but one of his enemies. Now, in 1803, the army was camped on the French coast, waiting for a chance to invade Great Britain. The British were relying on the Royal Navy, the most powerful fleet in Europe, to keep Napoleon away. If the French managed to evade the Royal Navy, or to divert its forces for even a few days, they could land an army in England.

To prevent a French landing, the British constructed a line of 73 unusual towers along their southern coast. They were based on a Corsican tower that the British had attacked nine years before. That tower had been bombarded by two warships with a total of 106 guns. With only three guns to defend itself, it managed to drive off both British warships. The secret was its walls. Because they were thick, circular, and sloped outward, the British cannonballs simply bounced off. This attracted the attention of British engineers, who were so amazed by the result that they decided to copy the design. They spaced their towers 450 to 550 m (500 to 600 yards) apart, so they could defend each other with their guns.

However, the towers were never tested. No matter how hard they tried, the French couldn't manage to divert the British navy. Despite this, the towers were considered so promising that another 27 were built along the east coast of England.

In the next 50 years, similar towers were built all around Great Britain and overseas – in Australia, South Africa, and Canada. These unusual towers stood on guard for the British Empire all around the world.

THE GUN
A gun firing an 11 kg (24 pound) shot was mounted on the tower's flat roof. The gun could fire in any direction by rotating on a central pivot, which was usually made from an old gun barrel. A small hatch was built into the door to the roof so ammunition could be moved to the gun without the door being opened.

THE MAGAZINE
Ammunition for the gun was kept on the ground floor, along with stores of food and water. Since sparks might set off the gunpowder, all the metal used on this floor was copper (which sparks less than iron) and the lantern was placed behind a glass sheet (to catch any embers).

THE NAME
The original tower had been located at Mortella Point on Corsica, an island south of France. *Mortella* was corrupted to give the British fortifications their name – Martello towers.

THE ENTRANCE

The only entrance to the tower was on the main floor, 6 m (20 feet) above ground level. A ladder was needed to reach the door, and it could be pulled inside if the fort was attacked. Some towers were surrounded by a ditch and had a drawbridge instead of a ladder.

WALLS

The tower's outer wall, built of brick, was thicker on the seaward side than on the landward. In some towers the landward wall was extremely thin. If the tower was captured by the enemy, the British could then easily destroy it.

COAST DEFENSE BATTERY

An imposing mass of brick and stone, Fort Point mounted over 120 guns. It had been designed to outshoot anything that could sail, but now it was decaying and obsolete. Up and down both coasts of America, U.S. forts couldn't protect the harbors they had been built to defend. Times had changed, and if war broke out they would stand no chance against modern warships. Worried civilians demanded harbor defenses with up-to-date technology. Modern guns were more powerful. One of them could hurl a 680 kg (1,500 pound) shell (as heavy as 10 soldiers) over a mile, or punch through 1.2 m (4 feet) of solid iron. Two of them could replace 120 older ones. And fewer guns required a much smaller structure.

The front of this battery was a grassy slope with small bushes planted to camouflage it. Behind this slope was a concrete platform for the guns. They were mounted on a remarkable new invention, the disappearing carriage – which popped up to fire, then back down to reload. When the guns were lowered, the battery was invisible to observers at sea.

The gun batteries were not the only new elements in the defense of American ports. Mortar batteries, controlled minefields, and a new fleet were also built to protect the coast. It took 25 years to complete the extensive defenses, which protected 26 U.S. ports with 300 heavy guns. The batteries were never attacked, and were eventually abandoned in the 1950s.

OLD   NEW

Older fortifications had to be placed close to each other. The longer range of new guns meant batteries could be placed further from each other and protect more harbor.

INFANTRY DEFENSES
Unlike earlier forts, these batteries did not have complex defenses on their landward side. Instead, the battery was protected from the enemy by soldiers.

PROTECTION

The front of the battery was a gentle slope of earth, backed by concrete. The earth absorbed the impact of shells fired at the battery, but didn't splinter like bricks or stone.

DISAPPEARING CARRIAGE

The Buffington-Crozier disappearing carriage raised and lowered the gun to protect it from enemy fire while reloading.

It did this with a counterweight system. When the weight went down, the gun went up, like on a seesaw. When the gun was fired, it recoiled backwards and down, raising the weight again. A gun mounted on a disappearing carriage could fire once a minute.

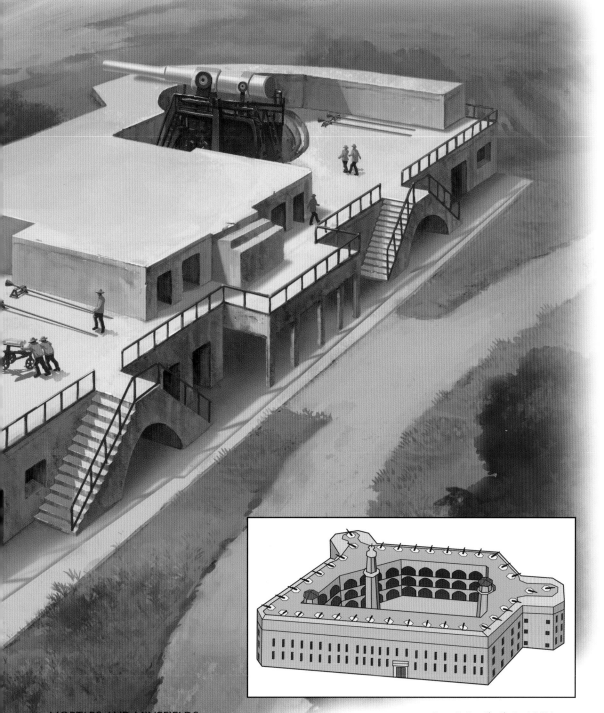

Fort Point (built in 1861) mounted over 120 guns in three tiers of casemates to defend San Francisco Harbor.

MORTARS AND MINEFIELDS

Using mortars to attack ships was a new idea. The mortars' plunging fire could hit the deck armor of an attacking ship, which was weaker than its side armor. In practice, it was harder to hit fast-moving ships with mortar fire than with guns.

Minefields were laid at the entrance to a harbor. They would be detonated from special observation points when an officer saw an enemy ship enter the minefield.

19

THE MAGINOT LINE

The French knew they would have to dig deep to protect their borders. During World War I, powerful artillery had destroyed the French and Belgian frontier forts. After the war, the French realized they would have to build much stronger defenses.

The new forts were buried deep underground. Only the guns were on the surface, protected by rotating metal turrets that could retract into the ground. The well-defended entrance to the complex was 3 km (1.8 miles) behind the gun positions, well away from the fighting. There was a cramped, damp underground barracks for the garrison. All the parts of this remarkable fort – guns, barracks, and entrance – were connected by a network of underground tunnels. A miniature electric train, called the *métro*, carried supplies like food and ammunition.

The French built 20 forts, placed close enough to protect each other. Smaller fortifications and mobile troops guarded the spaces between the large forts. Fortified houses on the frontier could warn of an attack, while heavy artillery behind the forts could fire right over them at the attackers. This impressive combination of defenses was called the Maginot Line.

The Line didn't run the entire length of the French border with Germany. There was a gap in the Ardennes Forest, where the trees were thought too dense to permit an invasion. The Germans disagreed, and successfully used it as an attack route during World War II. Avoiding most of the powerful forts of the Maginot Line, they struck deep into France. None of the forts were captured, and they only surrendered when the French government fell. The army had failed, not the forts.

GARRISON
In each fort lived 800 to 1,200 men. They were divided into four shifts called *watches*, like on a ship. One watch stood guard and manned the guns while the other three ate or slept. Because the Maginot Line was considered so important to the defense of France, its troops were the very best.

TURRET

WEAPONS
The armament of an average fort was:
- 6 75-mm (2.9-inch) guns
- 2 81-mm (3.2-inch) mortars
- 3 anti-tank guns
- over 10 lighter mortars
- over 50 machine guns

BARRACKS

The troops' barracks (shown in cutaway) had everything the garrison needed to live underground: storerooms, kitchens and washrooms, a hospital with an operating room, even a tiny one-cell jail. Soldiers slept in triple bunk beds, and only the commanding officer had his own room. Because space was so cramped, during peacetime the majority of the men lived in camps on the surface.

DEFENSES

The roof of each fort was 3.5 m (11 feet) of concrete covered by up to 20 m (66 feet) of soil (as tall as a five-story building). This was supposed to be invulnerable to even the heaviest artillery. A line of vertical steel posts kept tanks away, and a deep field of barbed wire did the same for infantry. If enemy soldiers did manage to climb on top of a fort, the adjacent forts could shoot at them without fear of damaging the fort underneath.

BARRACKS

Germany

Maginot Line

France

POISON GAS

The French designed their forts to be well protected against any threat – including poison gas. A special system controlled the air pressure in the forts to keep dangerous gases out.

FORT DRUM

They were called the "kings of the seas." At the start of the 20th century, the battleship was the most powerful weapon in any country's navy. Its guns could inflict tremendous damage on anything within 13 km (8 miles) of the coastline. Protecting a port meant being able to defeat a battleship.

The Americans captured the Philippines from the Spanish in 1898. To protect the Philippine capital, Manila, the Americans built forts on the four small islands that block the entrance to Manila Bay (Corregidor, Cabillo, Carabao, and El Fraile). Each island had heavy guns and controls for the minefields that ran between the islands. The smallest, and most unusual, fort was built on El Fraile island.

It took U.S. Army engineers 10 years to level El Fraile right down to the waterline and construct a concrete fort that covered the whole island. It had exterior walls 18 m (60 feet) thick (wider than a four-lane highway) and a roof reinforced with steel. The fort's main armament was four 14-inch (356 mm) guns mounted in a pair of turrets, just like those on a battleship. The rotating metal turrets meant the guns were well protected and gave them a wide field of fire. The shape of the fort, combined with its turrets, made it look a lot like a ship. In fact, although its official name was Fort Drum, it was usually called "the concrete battleship."

During the Second World War, the Japanese invaded the Philippines. They didn't think they had a chance against the island forts, so they came ashore much further north and had to struggle through the jungle to attack Manila from the landward side. After five months, the troops in the four island forts were the only Americans in the Philippines still resisting.

The forts were surrounded, with no hope of relief. Once the Japanese gained a foothold on Corregidor, the largest island, the forts surrendered. In spite of heavy aerial and artillery bombardment, Fort Drum's guns continued firing until the moment of surrender.

Manila
Manila Bay
Corregidor Island (FORT MILLS)
Cabillo Island (FORT HUGHES)
El Fraile Island (FORT DRUM)
Carabao Island (FORT FRANK)

Manila Bay, the Philippines

FIRE CONTROL
Fort Drum's guns were aimed from the top of a mast 18 m (60 feet) tall, like the one on a battleship. The height of the mast increased the range at which targets could be spotted. Rangefinders on the mast determined the range, speed, and direction of the target. This information was sent to the plotting room, on the lowest level of the fort, which gave instructions to the gunners in the turrets on where to aim.

THE GUNS

A Two 14" (356 mm) guns in each of a pair of turrets, called Battery William L. Marshall and Battery John M. Wilson.
B Four 6" (152 mm) guns in two-story casemates along the sides.
C A pair of 3" (76 mm) anti-aircraft guns on the roof of the fort.

The gun turrets were armored with 18" (45 cm) of metal on the front and 14" (36 cm) on the sides.

BARRACKS

Fort Drum had three floors. The garrison of 200 men slept on the top level and ate on the middle one. The lowest level was below the waterline even at low tide. It was reserved for the engine room (to power the turrets and lights), fuel and water tanks, and the plotting room (see Fire Control). Because the quarters in Fort Drum were so cramped (like a ship at sea!), during peacetime the garrison lived mostly in temporary wooden buildings constructed on the roof of the fort.

TODAY

The decaying hull of Fort Drum still stands in Manila Bay. Most of the metal has been sold for scrap.

23

CONTINENTAL DEFENSE

The threat of nuclear war hung over the United States of America. In 1950, the world had two superpowers: the capitalist democracy of the U.S.A. and the Communist USSR (also called Russia). Political arguments had brought them close to war. These tensions were called the Cold War, and America feared that a real war would soon occur – starting with a Soviet surprise assault on American cities.

The Russians could only attack the U.S.A. with the awesome power of atomic weapons by sending their jet bombers over the North Pole. To stop them, the Americans and their Canadian allies created a complex defensive network. Radars in the Far North would detect Soviet bombers, and American fighter planes would be guided to them by a sophisticated computer system called SAGE. SAGE was designed to identify enemy aircraft, direct U.S. fighters towards them, tell the fighters when to fire their missiles, then direct them back to their bases. The computer was even supposed to fly the plane, with the pilot in control only during takeoff, landings, and emergencies.

Even while American scientists worked on SAGE, a new threat appeared. In 1957, the Soviets launched the first satellite, Sputnik, into orbit. American commanders worried that the rocket that had put Sputnik in orbit could also drop a bomb on an American city. Rockets carrying nuclear bombs, called ballistic missiles, moved so fast they were almost impossible to destroy. They certainly made manned bombers obsolete.

At first, the Americans tried to build defenses that could stop the rockets. The Nike-Zeus missile was designed to hit and destroy an incoming ballistic missile with its

SAGE
The Semi-Automatic Ground Environment (SAGE) was a computer system designed to direct U.S. fighter planes. Each of the 24 SAGE computers weighed over 250 tons (226,800 kg) and generated so much heat that if the air conditioning failed, the computer would melt in 60 seconds. Although they were some of the most powerful computers at the time, a home computer today is more than 5,000 times as powerful. The U.S. Air Force designed a brand new fighter to work with SAGE, called the F-106 Delta Dart (because of the shape of its wings).

NIKE-ZEUS

This was the last of a series of American air defense missiles named for Greek gods (Zeus was the king of the other gods and Nike the goddess of victory). Designed to destroy enemy ballistic missiles, the Nike-Zeus had a nuclear warhead so it could destroy its target even with a near miss. One radar tracked Nike-Zeus's target while another tracked the intercepting missile. Computers on the ground automatically compared the information, then gave the Nike-Zeus missile commands by radio.

DEFENSE SUPPORT PROGRAM (DSP)

Orbiting 35,000 km (21,750 miles) above the earth, the DSP satellites use infrared sensors to detect the heat of a rocket engine. They send their information to ground stations in the United States. Although DSP satellites were never needed to detect missiles launched against the United States, they were used during the First Gulf War (1990–91) to detect Iraqi Scud missiles launched at Saudi Arabia and Israel.

25

NOT TO SCALE

own nuclear warhead. But U.S. planners realized there were too many Soviet missiles and bombers that would have to be stopped.

America changed its strategy to one called Mutually Assured Destruction (MAD). Increasing the numbers of its missiles and bombers, the U.S. pointed out that any Soviet attack would lead to retaliation that would destroy the USSR. It was thus in nobody's interest to attack. For MAD to work, the Americans had to be able to detect a Soviet attack and launch their own nuclear bombs in response. Otherwise, the Soviets might try to launch first, destroying the U.S. before it could respond. To provide the early warning, U.S. satellites orbiting over Russia employed infrared sensors to detect Soviet missile launches.

Scientific advances encouraged the U.S. president to change strategies in the 1980s. Using new technologies such as lasers and particle beams, he thought it would be possible for America to build defenses that could stop all Soviet nuclear weapons. President Reagan called his new plan the Strategic Defense Initiative (SDI), nicknamed Star Wars.

The Cold War between America and Russia ended before Star Wars was complete. In fact, the plans were far too ambitious to have succeeded. Defending the U.S.A. against ballistic missiles remained a dream, not a reality.

Military scientists continue to develop new ways to protect and defend.

STAR WARS
For the Star Wars program, American scientists explored a variety of possible ways to destroy enemy missiles. Among them were: laser satellites (shown here), lasers on the ground bounced off giant orbital mirrors, ground-based missiles, and the very "sci-fi"–sounding particle beam. None of these systems was ever developed to a usable level.

SIEGE DEFENSES

The defenders in their fortifications aren't the only ones who need protection. Attackers have always used protective devices rather than risk being caught in the open.

Archers and gunners preferred to work behind some sort of shield when shooting at forts and castles. One-man shields that stood on their own were called *pavises*, and were so useful that they were sometimes used in battles in open fields too. Larger wooden shields were called *mantlets*. These often had holes in them for the besieger to fire through.

The ancient Chinese had a particularly inventive version of the mantlet. A large wooden shield was hung from the end of a pivoted arm that was attached to a small wagon. The shield could be adjusted by moving the other end of the arm, while the wagon allowed it to be moved to any part of the attack.

Siege engines that had to be pushed against the wall, like *battering rams*, needed better protection because of their proximity to the enemy. A defender on the top of the wall could shoot arrows or toss stones onto them, killing the operators or damaging the machine. For protection, the siege engines were usually built with a wooden roof covered in wet animal hides. While the wood underneath would burn if the enemy hit it with fire, the wet hides stopped the flames from spreading.

The invention of the cannon spelled the end for these wooden protections. A cannonball could splinter a wooden screen without any trouble. Earth was more resilient than wood, so Renaissance (16th-century) besiegers dug trenches and protected their sides with *gabions* – woven baskets filled with earth.

Today, armies still use the same protections that Renaissance armies introduced: trenches, just like in earlier times, and sandbags, the descendant of the Renaissance gabion.

Mantlets shielded archers from enemy arrows.

Chinese mantlets could be pivoted to protect attackers from any direction.

This battering ram is covered in wet hides to prevent the enemy from setting it on fire.

BODY DEFENSES

The most basic forms of protection safe-guarded the human body: a helmet for the face, skull, and ears; a *cuirass* to guard the torso; simple *greaves* for the legs; a shield to block sword-blows or arrows. Together, they made up a suit of armor.

The effectiveness of the suit depended on a number of factors. How strong was the material? Leather was weakest, bronze better, and iron the strongest. Did it cover the entire body – even the joints, a common weak point? Was it light and flexible enough to fight in? A soldier in lighter armor could evade one wearing heavier or clumsier protection.

Some armies developed ways to increase protection by grouping soldiers together. The ancient Greeks took their basic set of bronze armor (helmet, cuirass, greaves, and a large shield called a *hoplon*) and made it part of a larger system. In the formation called the *phalanx*, each soldier was protected by three shields: his own and those of the men on either side. Working together, they were all better protected.

The Roman legionaries used a similar formation, the *testudo* (tortoise), when approaching enemy fortifications. The soldiers at the front and sides of the group pointed their shields outward, while those towards the inside raised their shields above their heads. Everyone was thus protected from arrows or stones coming from any direction.

Early warriors protected themselves with a cuirass, helmet, greaves, and shield.

A Greek phalanx presented a solid front of shields.

Armor got much heavier during Europe's Middle Ages. Eventually a mounted knight's armor, made from plates of solid metal, covered his entire body. Even his horse was armored. But the fully armored knight soon became obsolete, his protection useless and cumbersome once the use of firearms spread. These revolutionary weapons could penetrate all but the heaviest armors. Soldiers began to use only their steel breastplate, the most effective part, and eventually abandoned even this.

Armor returned in World War I, when metal helmets were issued to protect men from shell fragments. In World War II, some pilots began wearing *flak jackets* – cloth jackets with metal plates sewn in. This protected them against bullets that could penetrate the airplane. The metal in the jackets was too heavy for an infantryman who fought on foot.

In the 1980s, technology finally created armor that was light and flexible enough for every soldier. Kevlar is a light bulletproof fiber up to five times stronger than steel, and is used today to make bulletproof vests and helmets.

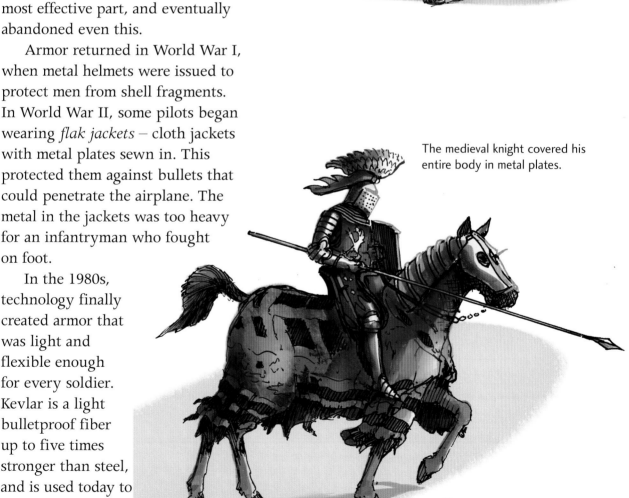

The Roman testudo protected the soldiers from four directions: front, both sides, and above.

The medieval knight covered his entire body in metal plates.

CAMOUFLAGE

In the 18th and 19th centuries, the time of muskets and cavalry, armies needed to wear brightly colored uniforms so they could recognize friends and foes on the battlefield. Around the turn of the century, the development of longer-ranged weapons, like rifles and artillery, meant soldiers no longer fought face to face and were able to spread out and take cover. Armies started using drab colors like khaki or gray to make their uniforms harder to see.

This soldier's uniform is khaki to blend in with the earth.

In World Wars I and II, camouflage was used on objects as well as men. Nets covered in strips of green and brown cloth were used to cover guns, supplies, vehicles, and headquarters – making them invisible from the air.

Variations in weather and lighting made it harder to disguise ships at sea. *Dazzle painting* was intended to break up the ship's shape, making it tough to tell what type of ship it was or what direction it was headed.

Dazzle painting uses black and white stripes to disrupt the ship's profile.

As soon as aircraft were used in war, air forces began to make use of camouflage. The airplane's lower side was painted in light tones, to blend in with the sky, and the upper side in darker tones that looked like the ground.

After World War II, armies had to camouflage themselves against things other than the human eye. Modern aircraft are covered in special material that absorbs radar waves, and they also use cooling fans and baffles to stop missiles homing in on their hot exhaust.

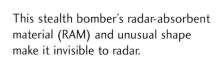

This stealth bomber's radar-absorbent material (RAM) and unusual shape make it invisible to radar.

TANKS

It's relatively easy to protect yourself when defending, but how do you protect yourself on the attack? In the 20th century, the answer was the tank.

The first tanks were developed during World War I (1914-18) as a way to safely attack enemy positions. The tank was invulnerable to rifle fire and machine guns, while its weapons could destroy the enemy.

Tanks were even more vital in the next war, World War II (1939-45), where they were one of the most important weapons on the battlefield. They remain valuable weapons today.

The earliest tanks had flat sides made from thin steel plate. In World War II, armor became much thicker (up to 180 mm/7 inches) and was sloped so that shells would bounce off.

Technological advances after the war necessitated new materials for tank armor. Chobham armor used alternating layers of ceramic (like a flowerpot) and steel to stop the jet of liquid metal a High-Explosive Anti-Tank (HEAT) shell uses to cut through a tank. Some tanks were fitted with Explosive Reactive Armor (ERA). These blocks of explosives were fastened to the outside of the tank and blew up enemy shells upon contact. The newest tanks use computerized active protection systems. These detect approaching anti-tank missiles with radar, then shred them with a small mortar round from a launcher on the side of the turret.

World War I tanks were the only vehicles that could cross "no man's land" without being destroyed.

Modern tanks use computerized active protection systems to defend themselves from missiles.

31

INDEX